# God's Intangible Senses

## DEBORAH HOUSEHOLDER

WESTBOW
PRESS
A DIVISION OF THOMAS NELSON
& ZONDERVAN

WestBow Press books may be ordered through booksellers or by contacting:

WestBow Press
A Division of Thomas Nelson & Zondervan
1663 Liberty Drive
Bloomington, IN 47403
www.westbowpress.com
1 (866) 928-1240

ISBN: 978-1-4908-6869-1 (sc)
ISBN: 978-1-4908-6870-7 (e)

Library of Congress Control Number: 2015903397

Print information available on the last page.

WestBow Press rev. date: 4/17/2015

The best and most beautiful things in the world cannot be seen or even touched. They must be felt with the heart.
—Helen Keller

# Contents

God Knows If You're Experiencing or Sensing…

# 1

# A Bullet through the Heart

Heartbreak can feel as if a bullet has gone straight through an aching heart. After a loss of someone or an idea, you may experience "wide-open" chest pains, and it may be the darkest time in your life. Your soul may scream, and the damage seems like a deep, dark canyon. You may feel unable to return to a "normal" life.

A hole in your heart and being may trigger deep regrets and emotional grief. It can feel as if a branding iron has had contact with your already raw, throbbing heart. You may have unwillingly participated in one of life's many trials. Often, you will reminisce or quiz yourself about what could have been or what could have been done differently. Just watching a simple television program or a listening to a shared familiar song seems roar out of that insensitive TV or radio. It brings back bittersweet moments of when you were once one.

Tender emotions create a darkness in your destroyed world. It's as if the blinds have been pulled down in your own heart. Everyone says that time will ease the ache, and it will make you stronger. As you experience this turmoil, though, there are no words or hugs big enough to stop the feeling of a bullet through a suffering heart.

# 2

## A Chunk of Coal or a Diamond in the Rough?

*Y*ou may feel as if you are only a chunk of coal, but hopefully you also have self-worth—fearless feelings of being a diamond in the rough. Often, you must let go of the old mental self-image and hold your shoulders back and head high. This will create a sense of deserving that you must have to be valued as an individual. Don't take the "poor me" attitude and set booby traps for your gullible mind, leaving it in the danger zone. Sure, we all make mistakes in this journey of life, but turn those lesson-learned mistakes into proud personal merits.

Sometimes, the weaknesses in your life can prove to be the strongest you have ever have been. Be your own best friend and stop throwing yourself a "pity-party" that leaves you empty and unsure. That's when the Devil makes sure he gets a personal invitation. Uneasiness, worry, fear, insecurity, and weakness all are "party favors" that the Devil brings to the one who is hosting the party. With our Lord's help, though, you can learn to love yourself again. It's your chance to sparkle in the sunlight and be all you can be. This will make you realize that you really are a diamond in the rough and not just a chunk of coal.

# 3

# A Clear Image and Mind-Set

A clear image and mind-set is what is genuinely needed to possess determination. Do not ever choose to give in or to let the "bad guy" creep into your thoughts. "I can't" should not be in your vocabulary or lifestyle. Staying positive and not letting the snowfall bombard the "big picture" with a devastating accumulation—that is a wise choice. Change your weaknesses into your strengths. Be the strongest and most potent person you have ever been. Your eyes and mind must stay focused on the prize ahead.

Staying firm and solid on an idea may not always be light and easy. You may have to endure an abundance of blood, sweat, and tears. Keep your goal always in sight, and never say, "Well, that's good enough." That will eventually pull the best out of you. Fear and intimidation are not welcome company to keep. Going the distance, however far, will get you to your goal.

You may experience weariness after an exhausting run, but that's the only way to the finish line. Having a short break can help you to endure the challenge. But having a clear image and mind-set will offer you a fixed purpose in life and the staying power to go all the way, even through adversity.

# 4

## A Knife That Stabs Pain through the Heart

Missing someone or something often feels as though a knife has been stabbed through the heart. God's timing, though, will heal all steady, constant pain. He knows precisely the time that you are prepared to replace the one named thing you miss the most. You may cry or call out for help, while having one of the darkest time of your life, but He does listen. His timing will be exact. Waiting on the Lord to breath "life" into you when you are struggling is all a timely process. You may wonder sometimes if we will ever be happy again, feel at ease again, or feel a warm touch again. Will the mournful tears ever stop?

Your heart may feel like you are pulling up the anchor on a already out-of-control vessel. An aching heart or a longing for something or someone may cause the body to fight, resulting in damaging depression or ideas. Sorrows of life will eventually catch up to you, though, even if you run. Life may not have turned out according to your plans, but running scared and having an ugly heart sure doesn't make the sun want to shine.

Your demons can often be yourself at times. Throw those harmful feelings out the window, get a hug for the lonesome soul, and pull that knife straight out of your heart because there will be life at the end of the tunnel.

# 5

## A Positive Route

*A* grief-stricken family must remember a loved one in a positive way, or route. Sure, there will be questions; such as, did the person suffer? Why did the loved one have to endure so much while still on this crazy, mixed-up planet? Some people prefer to be quietly left alone, while others rely on another mourning soul. Still others have faith in our loving God and know that they are in good hands. We must let go and realize that no matter what the circumstances were here, our loved one's skies are clear and blue now.

Acceptance of someone's death will be difficult, though. Of course, we must mourn, and our dear loved one will extremely missed. We must believe that our cherished one made his or her life count and instilled some of his or her life lessons into us. Remembering this will somehow help ease the pain. Our deceased loved one will experience only happiness and bliss for the soul hereafter.

Gifts from heaven are presented to the survivors in mysterious ways—in so-called coincidences. Our loved ones are very content to worship our Creator forever and to reunite with the loved ones who went before them. Never forget that they are angels on the other side, looking over us to make sure that we don't stumble.

We must keep our minds open and have a "positive route," because that will keep us going on the right path. One sweet day, we will all be together with our loved ones we have missed so desperately.

# 6

## A Trunk Full of Regrets

Having a trunk full of regrets can often make the soul begin to scream. Allow yourself to dance in the sun, and throw away all feelings of guilt out the window. Blaming yourself for committing or allowing any wrongdoings can make you run scared or fight yourself internally. Weigh the pros and cons, and be really and truly honest with yourself.

You may feel powerless, but actually it's the fear and worry that haven't a lick of power. We all make choices that we must live with, but don't become embittered and sink down deep into the quicksand. Don't focus on your faults and wave the surrender flag, because guilt can turn into ugly anger and flooding tears.

Guilt, however, also may create an undying willpower and hope for a better future. So forgive all the criminal offenses and let them go, like a helium-filled balloon to a clear blue sky. Be the "president" of your own life, and take up the badge of courage. None of us gets out of this life alive, so ask our heavenly Father for forgiveness—and forgive yourself too. Guilt can give you a trunk full of regrets, so take the lock off that trunk, and set yourself free from the heavy chains.

# 7

## All That and a Bag of Chips

"All that and a bag of chips" is the identity of people who are full of themselves and extremely arrogant. Image is everything to them, and they are very careful of the choices they make to ensure they don't stain that perfect perception. They check their mirrors often to make sure that every little hair is in place or that the name brand label is visible. "Me, me, me" is the only conversation from such selfish people. They will never let their guard down, for fear of letting someone to see inside or that they are human.

Vain thoughts or actions can often come rushing out. These people do not care if they step on someone else's heart in the process. Stuck-up friends snicker at others if they don't quite fill their group's criteria. Crippled pride jumps off their skin, giving an intolerable, foul odor. An overbearing manner reveals a conceited persona and big-headedness.

What genuinely needs to be remembered and considered is, what if the shoe were on the other foot? No one needs to be judgmental because absolutely nobody is "all that and a bag of chips."

# 8

## *Alone Time with the Maker*

Dedicate valued time alone with the Maker. Believing you will continue to breath in and out, you will wake up to smell the dew-kissed morns, and you will feel the sweet pitter-pat of your musical chest are all examples of an appreciated faith. Faith is a quality that you cannot smell or touch. Fighting the good fight of faith can be extremely rewarding, especially when you can feel the Devil staring, watching, and laughing at any misfortunes that happen in your life. The soul longs terribly for and seeks truth and fairness.

Faith is trusting God with your life and knowing that He will forgive you if you truly are sorry for your behavior, actions, or foolishness. Unseen are the many acts of kindness He performs for each and every one of us daily. Blessings are directly from the "big guy," and sometimes they feel undeserved.

Understanding that there is a greater power, a Maker of heaven and earth (the entire universe, for that matter), is something you can feel proud about knowing. Prayers are not just a waste of your energy, mouth, or thoughts.

Lifting your prayers up to the Savior and letting Him handle them in His own manner and His own time is also called patience. Treasuring alone time with the Maker should be considered a gem and should never, ever be taken for granted.

# 9

## *An Erupting Volcano*

Anger can build and bubble up until it bursts out like an erupting volcano, flowing out to destroy anything in its path. Your body will begin to tremble and shake when that raging emotion erupts. Hostility showers down, covering all the healthy vegetation that has been planted. Cruel thoughts and untamed words roar at an innocent by-stander. Inflamed, emotional actions create a mess of sanity. Unfriendly manners irritate others, as this raging inferno takes over a helpless body.

This menacing aspect can ruin an otherwise fantastic day. Frowns appear everywhere, due to lack of kindness. Mean looks and expressions portray a confused soul. Unfavorable results will most likely occur.

Some of life's crises require a calm, composed spirit to prevent a dormant volcano from erupting suddenly.

# 10

## Undercover Angel

An "undercover angel" displays natural grace and effortless charm. A warm-hearted smile is always an elegant awakening that radiates from a glistening glow. Kindness and courtesy are pleasing and respectful characteristics. An undercover angel will offer overflowing compliments for needy souls and exhibit a friendly nature. He or she will possess a listening, empathetic ear and an understanding heart. Harmony and mercy are in perfect unity. An awe for nature and a gentleness toward life itself are forever traits of an undercover angel.

An undercover angel shows dignity and care in daily living. A lovable and joyous disposition is another honorable feature of an undercover angel. This type of person holds a positive outlook, which returns only positive effects and allows others to show a deep and complete approval. Saying "please," "thank you," and "excuse me" are respectable habits. An undercover angel usually accompanies a guiding spirit and follows all the ways of the higher power, as they partner side by side. Perhaps you have crossed the path of an undercover angel, unaware of his or her presence.

# 11

## Another Day in Paradise

Another day in paradise doesn't mean spending an additional day on an exotic island somewhere. No, not if you are grateful for every moment you are alive. Being thankful for your life, family, and faith can only teach you how to live and be joyous. What other choice do you have?

You could have an upside-down smile, love selfishly, and live silently. Where would you be then? None of us knows what lies ahead, so there is little time for pettiness.

Develop a brand new plan for potential problems. Always be glad, first and foremost, that your life is not the worst it could be. Thoughts of being the victim in every situation can make you feel lifeless and often can feel like the glass is always half empty.

Tricky bumps in the road must not detour you, and you should not make comparisons to others who may appear to "have it made in the shade." Be appreciative that the test results came back fine, that the baby was born healthy, and that the sun rises every glorious morn.

Be the first to bury the hatchet—forgive or accept others' downfalls. Angelically, your prayers have arrived, so be grateful because life is truly another day in paradise.

# 12

## Blessed Beyond Belief

Enchantingly, at that very moment when Jesus breathes life into us, we are blessed beyond belief. We owe it to our Savior to try our hardest to be all that we can possibly be. Our happiness cannot be purchased, borrowed, or even stolen. Staying positive and seeing all the possibilities, instead of all the sorrows, will have a dramatic effect on our lives. Moving mainly forward in our lives is the only direction to take. We need each other for support, and we must treat everyone as equals.

What can we do today to make someone else laugh and smile? We will feel truly blessed by serving others. We will be living the way God wants us to live. Planting good seeds of family faith and then reaping what has been sown is what life should be all about.

We are all just "works in progress," and if we are loyal and abiding to our God, everything else will fall into place. We must continue to keep smiling faces and try extremely hard not to be hard on ourselves. After all, we are truly blessed beyond belief!

# 13

## Christ on Your Face

Peace and tranquility appears on your face when your are full of Christ and of the Holy Spirit. Serenity can be as simple as a golden sunset, rain, tap-tap-tapping on a tin roof, or fluffy white snow hugging the ground on a family-filled Christmas Eve. It even can be a newborn kitten, with eyes tightly shut, as it feels the comfort and security of being with its mother. These offer a calm sense of peace and a soothing attitude.

No therapists or physologist are needed when you witness an eagle soaring against a mountaintop backdrop. Just imagine a quiet and still angel, candidly "chilling" up high on a cloud. Contentment and joy comes from within when you realize that your life could not be any more full of blessings and that all your prayers have been answered from up above.

Seeing clearly in color eases your mind that once fought an ugly dilemma. Clouds float across a crescent moon, as a pleased cricket sings a calming song. A precious loved one is sleeping with angels, after the sun has gone down after a battle with a terminal illness. Listening to a treasured song that floods the heart can bring back memories of a time when a shared bond was experienced with a unique individual.

Peace and Christ can especially be noticed on the face of a newborn child and on the child's parents, as they cradle the child with thankfulness. The brand new procreators have come to the realization that life has made a complete and perfect circle. Just take a quick look around, and it won't be too difficult to see a face that reflects the wondrous Christ.

# 14

## Count to Ten

$W$hen the water gets high, count to ten, even though it may be highly frustrating. You must be the "professional person." This type of person follows his or her spirit by not listening to evil thoughts and words. Being the bigger person will keep gruff words from flying and a negative attitude from getting unleashed. It is a choice and decision not to let wasteful anger "murder" someone else's positive day.

Life and its surroundings can be exceedingly trying on a faulty day, but be prepared for the knock of the Devil at the back door. Having a calm way of dealing with an aggravating problem will let you grow into a healthy and caring soul. Human impurities can draw on your energy and fester like a boil. Don't sink to the level of quicksand, never being able to return to the surface.

People and situations can push your buttons to the limits. Magnifying a difficulty only expands a puny problem into an immense one. Irritation and annoyances are a huge part of life but how you decide to act on them will reveal whether or not you are a kind-hearted person. Counting to ten allows time for all egos to settle before responding and rushing into an already flaming state.

# 15

## Daydreaming

𝓘 long to feel your perspiring skin against my own and stroke my eager hands through those beautiful locks. My crude mind rocks with desiring thoughts as I tremble, trying hard to settle my forbidden feelings. Why can't I just have you?

Oh, that's right—it would be the unethical thing to do. Daydreaming of our being together is allowed, though. Just the very thought of your familiar gentleness travels through my head, making my heart race faster. Will we be gentle and loving or be like two eager animals in their prime? All I know for sure is that my curious mind is working overtime, just thinking of you. Only spending time on your soft shoulder, using it as a pillow, will comfort this lonely body.

Desperately, I need a shower after we're together, but I detest the idea of having to wash the tantalizing scent of your sensual body off mine. I am dripping. Is it the water from the shower or just the wetness you leave me with? I imagine my breath on your neck as I nibble your irresistible ears that sport those manly earrings. Flirting with each other—with our laughter, teasing stares, and suggestive looks—makes me cream with excitement. Candlelight against your skin holds me deep in my dreams.

Suddenly, the telephone ring startles me and explodes my intense daydream of us.

# 16

## Cope with the Hand That is Dealt

$\mathcal{A}$cceptance can be extremely difficult to face when you are dealt a lousy hand. Bucking the system or breaking the man-made rules will only make it worse. It feels sometimes as if fighting gale-force winds is all you have accomplished.

God has already given us an exceptional hand—the gift of life. It's really up to us to play the cards wisely. Receive His many blessings with a gracious attitude or mind-set. Denial can be a cruel enemy, when refusing to acknowledge the awful truth or the way you would like your life to be. Forbidding the angels to take flight with your life can be like a boat without essential water.

Agreeing to take life as it is pitched to a player can only result in a homerun on the playing field of life. Moving along with the bustling traffic makes a long journey seem to speed by, as if a short mile. Praying for peace within yourself may be needed when a troublesome problem that cannot be mended occurs. Coping with a terminal illness or an extreme intensity of pain may make us try to bargain with God. Praying for strength and a means to deal with it may have to happen before acceptance finally occurs.

If it is possible, though, conquering and climbing that steep mountain makes the destination all the sweeter. Being dealt a good hand isn't always the name of the game. It's really how a player chooses to cope with the hand that is dealt that makes him or her the champion in life.

# 17

## Devil, Go Away!

A soul must shout, "Devil, go away!" when a pity party has been thrown and total darkness buries the spirit in a gloomy and depressed state. Calling out, as a coyote does at a glowing moon, we cry uncontrollable. With the lack of essential energy, we can withdraw from the world's activities. Bedtime becomes earlier and earlier, as we proclaim tiredness or exhaustion. Our baffled friends go by the wayside, as we have lack of interest in daily activities. Hopelessness becomes the most common and unwelcome feeling. The sun has gone down on a once pumping personality.

How long can a body endure this ache? Despairity sits heavy on a wide-open chest. Satan is among us. The wicked one is laughing at our sorrows. Rain falls from the heavens, as God cries for our bleakness. The tailed man plays complex games in our confused hearts and minds. Loneliness and simple boredom will allow the Devil an open door to play these mind games. We must continue to slam the door and shout, "Devil, go away!"

# 18

## Devil's Playground

Boredom can give the Devil time to amuse himself at the playground that was precisely built for him. Dullness of an inactive brain can allow this malicious man to bring a wasteland of thoughts. Father Time also offers continuous periods of agonizing and dragging weariness.

Time can be spent watching the squirrels as they climb head first down a tree, or even watching a daring bird who flies oh-so-close to your window, unaware of its curious spectator.

The complex mind can be a battlefield if left dormant. It can feel as though the body is imprisoned. Sweet and salty goodies become the suicide of choice. Repetitious favorite movies can be quoted word for word. When we are not challenged enough and our minds are wide open, looking for excitement, we had best prepare for trouble, as the never-ending clock ticks.

Time can heal a wound, though. It is not a nasty word to those who choose to keep the mind occupied. This way, there will be no hours left in the day for the Devil to wildly entertain himself at his malicious and unfair playground.

# 19

## Don't Leap from the Frying Pan into the Fire

Don't leap from the frying pan into the fire. Be loyal. The results of disloyalty can get you into a hot, sticky mess. Perhaps it's a broken marriage that has made a confused partner be unfaithful. Maybe someone is not being true to himself by not sticking with a diet or exercise plan. A selfish person suddenly gets discovered when he secretly steals from his unexciting company job. A once-devoted small-town grocery store patron gets spotted at another cut-throat, low-cost grocery warehouse.

Countries or governments must tremble with disappointment when they hear of treason. Man's best friend, the dog, always knows his owner's scent, voice, and schedule. Fish may wonder why it has been so quiet and peaceful in their pond, as the eager fisherman wanders off to a new fishing hole. A concerned family member believes in her loved one after a life-changing accident has left the loved one in rehabilitation for a spell. A friend must offer a rejection to a friend's spouse, who has confessed a hidden attraction.

Also, our Savior, Jesus Christ, wants an undying loyalty to Him. Remember, we need to sacrifice some of our selfish bad habits, but to every end is a beautiful new beginning. Take some alone time with Jesus. After that, you may not be tempted to leap from the frying pan into the fire.

# 20

## *Family*

$\mathcal{F}$amily is a magical connection with that special someone. His or her constant presence in our lives compares to none. Proper parents enlighten our faith and give us their wisdom. Concerned siblings assist us with our worries and perhaps dry our tears. Friends often act as family when we're down in the dumps. They will pull us up and out, and our gloomy mood may switch.

When we're all grown up and have families of our own, our lives often get very hectic, but we are never alone. "I am with you always" reads the Scripture of Matthew 28:20. In Him, we have our blessed family, and in Him we have plenty.

# 21

## *Freedom*

Our freedom rings when our armed forces fly overhead or when the colorful fireworks begin America's favorite sport, baseball. All the hoopla makes the heart swell with patriotism. Our sweet, sweet freedoms were paid for with the cost of many dedicated lives. Our loyal American soldiers gave their souls, so we could have it all—and then some. That is why we should never put a price tag on anything as precious as our freedom.

US citizenship carries a deeper value, as we recognize our red, white, and blue. We salute our flag, each stripe representing one of the first colonies, and a star for each state in the union. The eagles soar over our lands, which blooms our national flower, the rose. Our cracked Liberty Bell is still rung in Pennsylvania to this day, on the Fourth of July. Uncle Sam proudly listens as schools around the nation declare our Pledge of Allegiance.

Freedom, once again, is represented by the broken chains that lie beneath our welcoming Statue of Liberty's feet. George Washington would be flattered to see his face on the currency that is used daily by Americans. Respectfully, a twenty-one–gun salute and a folded American flag are embraced in honor of a hero who rests in peace at Arlington.

Always remember: we are one great nation, under God, and many sacrifices have been given for our precious freedom. Happy Fourth of July!

# 22

## God Is Crying

Hate is such an ugly, heavy word and emotion that can darken the sky as the rain pounds to the earth. With all due respect, this may make it seem as if God is crying. Our rocky relationship with others has made Him tear up, making lightning strike and thunder crash around us.

Just because someone does not follow our path, that doesn't mean we should detest the other person's way or actions. Being mean or hostile all the time toward someone can color our world dark with storm clouds. It can destroy our soul, make us struggle immensely, and possibly even ruin our sparkling, sunny day.

Disfavoring a person is perfectly fine, but when it becomes a huge turmoil in our lives, that's when it becomes very unhealthy. Our physical well-being, as well as our mental state, will be jeopardized. Not only that, but our bond with our Savior will be tarnished.

So next time you are tempted to despise or hate someone or something, just remember that it makes God sad. He doesn't approve, and He might show it by sending a rain shower.

# 23

## Hang in There!

Hang in there and be diligently patient, while waiting on the sun to rise. Experience all of the grace of its beauty setting in the west, also. Waiting for a seed to become a beautiful, healthy flower can often be a grueling task, but it must be done. Learning an appreciation for the moon and stars is a blessing, but one that may have to be endured to see a dawn of a new, gifted day.

Chickens all over the world must have endless patience to hatch their precious jewels. Successful bakers must also possess this patience to create the finest breads. Excited children really have a tough time delaying any longer than needed to find a toy-filled Christmas morn.

Remember the old cameras that snapped an instant photograph that everyone was dying to see develop right before their eyes? Time is not a bad or a curse word. Patience is our most difficult virtue, but good things happen to those who wait.

Keep your mind busy so you can achieve your goal and be the professional person. Just keep in mind that a man in the Bible named Job was tested many times and in many ways, but he hung in there and kept his faith and patience very well.

# 24

## *Heads Up, Shoulders Back!*

$\mathcal{S}$elf-confidence is extremely attractive. Holding your head high with your shoulders back shows self-assurance. Arrogance and big-headedness are not twins of confidence or even a close cousin. A feeling of certainty in the way you hold yourself will give others the same impression. A constant smile will shine a positive attitude and a firm opinion of yourself and most likely reflect a strong will. Being your own best friend can guide your ship safely off an unsettled sea.

Walking with a fearless pride shows poise and dignity as you swagger through the carnival of life. Others' opinions of you are really empty and pointless, if you smell the refreshing, natural, mountaintop air. Viewing yourself as a respectful and faith-filled person, a person of honor and conviction, maximizes the chances that others will stand that position.

Strive to be the most prime and choice person possible as you persevere through the wicked ways of this world, which can be cruel and unjust. Believing in yourself and being self-reliant and secure in who you are allows the grass to grow greener and fuller on your side of the fence. Character begins to blossom when, as a confident person, you trust your heart and use the good head that is on your shoulders.

Taking pride in yourself is not conceit; it is self-respect. Blue skies are ahead of you if you hold your head up and proudly put your shoulders back, as if to say to the world, "Here I am!"

# 25

## I'm in Love with Myself

$\mathcal{S}$aying that you are in love with yourself may sound arrogant, but having an unselfish, personal pride and dignity is a living example of the way God designed humans to be. Self-respect does not make you conceited, vain, or even full of yourself. Ask yourself daily what you can do today to make someone else's life easier or better. This must be a continuous thought in your mind.

Glorifying or worshiping yourself, though, is simply arrogance. Keep yourself clean and neat in appearance, and you will be poised to tackle anything. Confidence and being sure of yourself can bring only positive responses, and your life will follow that path. Certainty and being optimistic of the course that you are taking is a requirement you must be willing to make in order to be fully content.

Free-falling out of the sky, like a falling star, is not the answer. Be selective about the way you project yourself in appearance, attitude, and the you speak; this will be the best decision that you make. Feeling that you are in love with yourself can be a good thing but only if used in a way that glorifies God in the highest.

# 26

## Are You Really Breathing?

Are you really breathing if you take your life for granted and do not take full advantage of the opportunities that have gently been placed at your feet? Acting a little bit mischievous is permitted, as long as you are not in harm's way.

To truly feel alive, we must grant ourselves permission to have excitement and joy in our lives. Each day, it is our duty of faith to execute these spirited emotions. After all, God did breathe life into all of us. Being playful doesn't mean you can't take the world and all its contents seriously when need be. It shows our Lord and others that your life is not to be taken for granted and that that you really do believe that you are blessed beyond belief.

Sadness and depression are so very heavy; we need to just throw them out the window. Even though the sorrows of life can be trying, we must keep soaring like an eagle, loosen up, and relax. Having an upbeat attitude and a winning smile will make the Devil run as fast as he can travel in the opposite direction. Having an innocent, devilish laugh, though, can actually make you feel like you are sailing free through life. It will also keep your enemies, if there are any, guessing about why you are so happy!

Without even speaking a word, facial expressions can offer insight to what you truly are feeling. Prankish behavior (of the innocent and sinless kind) can make you feel as though you are breaking the man-made rules. These are the rules that release the inner child, making you feel young again. Simply smiling and laughing can make your trip in life a little more enjoyable.

If you stay positive, your life will most likely follow in the correct direction. So go ahead—allow yourself to be just a little bit mischievous each day and truly feel yourself breathe in and breathe out.

# 27

# It Can't Be Taken Back

Remember that you cannot ever take back harsh words or a regretful error that inflicts pain and anguish on someone. Morally, you should feel guilty and remorseful for the effects on someone else's life. Worthlessness and low self-esteem can be the consequences of poor judgment. Outcomes can be devastating and cause mental suffering. Misdeeds can make the thunder crash and make the angels give a fretful and disappointed sigh.

Grieving your mistakes is what truly should happen, as well as being sorrowful for any wrongdoings you've made to others. Sometimes, just trying to survive may be the genuine reason why you make life-changing decisions. But doing what is wrong can cause your stomach to churn, especially when the bottom drops out.

We must consider how others will perceive an action or a comment, as it will reflect a memory of us. Our goal should be to not create a memory of misery and evil. We need to make the right first impression because seldom are we granted a second chance. Our behavior models who the person genuinely is inside.

So be careful—those declarations you make can never be taken back, even if you are truly sorry for them.

# 28

## Just Another Battle Scar

After a pounding rain has settled, you might have to say that this wound will be chalked up as just another battle scar. It may seem as if the world is coming to an end if something or someone disappoints you. Your mind is constantly busy with worry and fear of what may be the outcome. If you let it ruin your birthday, though, by not letting other feelings, such as happiness and peace, float in your mind, what a waste and shame it would be.

Strength and endurance are found when you learn to deal with the abandonment of contentment. Expectations of what could happen or fretfully looking at an event may let you down; you could be asking for a heartache. Misleading information can set you up for disaster, and you must prepare for failure.

You can keep on trying and trying even harder, but if it's not in the Maker's plans, you must move forward. Dissatisfaction should not detour you, though, from believing in all the possibilities. You may be displeased with the way things have turned out, but let the sun continue to shine, even during a thunderstorm.

You eventually may wonder what you wished for, and you know that it was never meant to be. Everyone experiences disappointments from time to time in this unfair, crazy world. Some things, though, need to be chalked up to another battle scar in the battlefield of life.

# 29

## Learning to Dance in the Rain

Watching a potentially deadly storm pass by is something for which we should be extremely thankful, but we may just have to learn to dance in the rain until then. Thanksgiving Day is also an occasion we should all be grateful for such matters as our family, friends, health, and faith. Although a farmer may favor good weather, all days must be appreciated on this God-created earth. Becoming embittered by life's challenges or misfortunes can leave you feeling lonely, sour, and tart.

Instead, we first must always enjoy our successes, before we can truly learn from any of our failures that may be encountered. Showing gratitude for our plain, sometimes even boring lives may actually show us how to love, laugh, and learn more than ever could be imagined. Possibly, it may take acquiring how to live again. This is an art that few people ever get to experience, though.

Credit can be given to our heavenly Father for lending His helping hands. Like a rainbow's beauty and color, these wonders mysteriously appear right out of thin air. He also provides us the ability to dream, our tender emotions, and even our thought process. Watching the beauty of nature in its own environment, such as an eye-catching sunset or moonlit nights under a bed of stars also can be credited to our Master. On our slow and hum-drum days, though, we may just have to learn how to dance in the rain until the storm passes.

# 30

## Life at the End of the Tunnel

We must trust that there will be life at the end of the tunnel someday. We also must believe that the glorious sun will rise as we greet each new day with a "Morning, glory!" Having hope is somewhat the same faith. Wishing upon a shooting star gives us a vision of the longing desire coming true. Dreaming immensely will give us the wings of an angel. Miracles do happen, so dream with everything you have!

After a light rain shower, we imagine a colorful, promising rainbow, offering us an end with a new, fresh beginning. Everyone has a duty to see the unlimited possibilities, instead of the "ho-hum" problems. Soaring like an eagle, we anticipate our bright future, full of love, happiness, and belonging.

Being but a freckle, only a small part of this big ol' world, we should desire only to be at our prime all the time. Crossing our fingers cannot hurt, though. After all, unimaginable dreams have come true. Believe in God's glory and that He only wants the best for us. Where would we be if we didn't have that hope and believe there is life at the end of the tunnel?

# 31

## Nursing Home Blues

$\mathcal{S}$omeone wets his Depends, as his neighbor yells, "Bingo!"

Down the hall, a woman babbles a lot of gibberish, some other form of lingo.

Where the most commonly used words are *huh* or *what*, ah, the aroma in the air of a soiled butt!

Wheelchairs lined up next to each other, relentlessly waiting to be put to bed.

At other times, they are lined up in the hallway, anticipating, to get fed.

There is a business in the hall, especially if a frail individual happens to fall.

Confused, he will ask, "Where's my room?" or cry wolf by yelling, "Help! Help me!"

Some sleep right there in the hall, others are constantly in traffic's path, while others stay close to the bathroom, for fear they might have to pee.

Chronic complainers are frequently very cold.

I suppose that happens to a person when he gets old.

Blowing noses often occurs while eating a meal, and sometimes a petty argument gets aroused by a misunderstanding.

Oh boy, what a deal!

Nursing home blues can be humorous, if you don't let it get you down.

Who knows? It could be a priceless treasure, turning out to be a valuable gem.

# 32

## Oh, Thank God!

*O*n a relieved sigh, we may often say, "Oh, thank God!" Oh, thank God that the long-awaited test results came back negative. Oh, thank God that I passed that nerve-racking driving test. Oh, thank God that the inspirational speech I gave made a life-changing impression on my audience. Oh, thank God—it's Friday! Oh, thank God that I got a good yearly report from the dreaded dentist. Oh, thank God that the parched farm crops got a soaking rain shower. But oh, thank God that severe storm only dropped only much-needed rainfall. instead of hail, like predicted.

Oh, thank God that my child with a new driver's license arrived at his destination safely. Oh, thank God; I am so blessed to still have a vibrant and healthy family. Oh, thank God; the timely surgery went according to the doctor's plan. Oh, thank God that the job interview is finally over.

Oh, thank God; I received an awesome grade on that final exam. Oh, thank God that I got away from those potentially deadly drugs. Oh, thank God—I made it through another session of that sweat-rolling, heart-racing exercise workout. Oh, thank God that I discovered where I misplaced those doggone keys!

Oh, thank God that I had a very compassionate friend who could understand my complicated and complex problems. Oh, thank God; my children are doing all right after their father's untimely death.

Oh, thank God for everything, every day, every moment.

# 33

## Playing Hopscotch with the Devil

*J*ealousy is a game of tearing up a conflicted heart or a form of suicide to one's own complex emotions. It eats up value time and precious energy that can never be returned. Perhaps this is like playing hopscotch with the Devil himself. Self-doubt and uneasiness are surrendered to that man with horns. Fear and worry are really are powerless if a soul is blissfully content. Dark clouds of negativity will form over a sorry, weak soul that fails to make a best friend with his or her own self.

Being envious of objects, physical looks, or a so-called marvelous relationship are exclusive traits of the man who wears red and fashions a long tail. Insecurities in life can bring feelings of loneliness and a deep cry for sympathy, if anyone will even listen anymore. Tears for or whimpering thoughts of what someone else possesses are empty.

Swallow hard, zip your trap, and rip up your own pride. That won't always come easily, but if security and love for yourself is on the table, playing hopscotch with the Devil should never be an option.

# 34

# *Put Our Big-Girl Pants On*

We must learn how to put our "big-girl pants" on and not be afraid of that big ol' boogieman! Be courageous and go looking for that deformed, ugly guy! We must learn to go the distance with any adversity with which our lives have been broadsided. Be totally fearless because fear only creates negativity.

All challenges and threats must be met head-on. We ought to free-fall into the adventures of life like a suspenseful mystery, only discovering pieces of the puzzle as we get closer to the prize. If we are never bold or adventurous, we can never reach that untouched mountain.

See only the possibilities, not the pointless problems. Don't let the dark clouds block the beautiful sunshine and view of the sun. Getting back up after life has kicked us hard in the stomach may be the most difficult and bravest triumph of our lives. It won't be easy, though.

It takes fearlessness to look that Devil square in the eye. Tell him that he's not given a fair fight. Go for the gusto! Dream big and never let the spirit cower.

Fear is just a small four-letter word. Just listen to the strong and steady voice inside. Leave all fears and anxieties behind, be steadfast, and don't let the Devil have any leverage. So let's put on our big-girl pants and go stalking that big ol' boogieman.

# 35

## Put Our Trust in God

Curiosity really did kill the cat, but we desperately need to put our trust in God nowadays. Quizzing our unknown future? Put our trust in God. Believe in horoscopes? Put our trust in God. Will the wicked storm attack our quiet neighborhood? Put our trust in God. When will we ever lay our heads on that special someone's shoulder? Put our trust in God.

Interested in the quantity and quality of lives we may have? Put our trust in God. Eager to know how our poverty-stricken life may change after winning the lottery? Put our trust in God. Probing to hear the latest, hot gossip? Put our trust in God.

Will the forecasted weather be trustworthy for a much-needed vacation? Put our trust in God. Will we suffer at all when it comes our time to die? Put our trust in God. After saving money throughout our lives, will our family be taken care of financially? Put our trust in God. Are we concerning ourselves with whether or not we will get that promotion at work? Put our trust in God.

How will our daughter ever raise her child alone in this mixed-up world? Put our trust in God. Can we ever change a extremely bad habit that has swallowed us whole? Put our trust in God. Will a expensive counselor be able to save our rocky marriage? Put our trust in God.

Will the hole in our hearts ever heal after our child's sudden death? Put our trust in God. Will our unmanageable debt ever be under control? Put our trust in God. Is our utility bill more than we can pay? Put our trust in God. Will the farm crops ever be able to survive this sweltering heat? Put our trust in God. Can we bear the hurtful, untrue rumors that are getting out of hand? Put our trust in God.

You and I will have all the answers to our lives if we only will put our trust in God.

# 36

## Sharpest Tool in the Shed?

It turns out that simple common sense is not as common as once thought. Being born with a familiarity with the world is a quality that is often taken for granted. Exceptional parenting skills also can play a tremendous part as well. Intelligence doesn't necessarily give someone the one thing needed to function successfully in this world: common sense. We can only imagine that some have purchased their bargain "intellect card" at a second-hand store. Getting the real gist of it is not on the daily menu for someone who thinks that studying is a must for a blood test.

Knowing when to shut your mouth and when to speak to show a backbone is a great example of society-learned common sense. Also, a waitress should have enough common sense that when she brings a massive plate of French fries, she brings a bottle of ketchup along as well. Some of the stupidest comments can come out of a senseless person's mouth because of lack of thought processing. We can't help but wonder if some people use a food processor for their brain instead of a thought processor. Why set a table for six when only five can comfortably fit?

Blondes everywhere are greatly offended at the silly jokes, when it's really the other hair colors that have given the blondes their notorious name. Some people speak the universal language of "smelly garbage," but they are unaware of their own blemish. Being the "sharpest tool in the shed" is not a matter of life, but it sure helps in this complicated journey that they call life.

# 37

## Skeletons in the Closet

Sometimes human fear and hidden skeletons in the closet can make your head spin uncontrollably. Trying to keep a secret can be a full-time job in itself. Fears and worries will have little potency when you gives them up to our Savior, though. There is no sense in worrying yourself into a tizzy. Just let it be because what will happen, will happen, regardless of the amount of sleepless nights you endure.

Running scared can prevent you from seeing the brightest color in a God-sent rainbow or perhaps the smiling face of an angel sent straight from the heavens above. If a privacy is shared with another, we may wish we could backtrack and have a "do-over." Sometimes people who have had a disgraceful past do not want any of the remnants of it in their lives. They will climb the highest mountain or seal themselves securely into a mason jar, so no one can see the drama in their lives.

Tears of shame may fall like rain on occasion, which can help ease the pain. There is nothing shameful about an occasional shower here and there. How you choose to accept your moment in the spotlight truly determines your spirit. Letting shame color your world can make you a cold and bitter individual.

Choosing to stay positive and offer up any regrets will create a more healthy and smiling soul. When you stand at the pearly gates of heaven, God will not judge you for others' mistakes. Trust that He knows all about your skeletons in the closet.

# 38

## *Stormy Situation*

Being stubborn possibly can create a stormy situation. Standing firm on a subject can cause an abundance of storm clouds to form, if you choose the wrong approach. Rough and inclement weather can be the consequences of a bad choice that will have to be lived with. Stop thinking of being the victim. Having an unchanging view of circumstances can have a windy and blustery effect on people, if used in an incorrect way.

On the other hand, stubbornness can be a good course to follow. Being hard-headed can help you go the extra mile. Living with a set opinion can make you travel the distance, especially in a difficult situation. If you are forced to, use adversity as a tool. Existing with an inflexible idea may be a means of survival.

Solid images can project a feeling of mind over body, creating an amazing form of obstinacy. So instead of bringing stormy situations to the table, go forth with the stubbornness, but bring a beautiful, breathtaking rainbow, if possible.

# 39

## *Superhero*

$\mathcal{D}$o you possess all the qualities of a superhero and often are seen as an inspiration and a survivor? Perseverance and having a positive dream will allow you to have power over fear and obstacles. This leaves you to be thought of as a superhero in someone else's eyes and mind.

Our darkest times should not a time to run for shelter. Learning how to "dance in the rain" will earn you a badge of courage, as you suck it up and put on your big-girl pants. Sure, there will be tears shed and lonely times every now and then, and yeah, life may not have taken the path that it was intended.

But when that doubting voice inside is heard, develop a new positive stand toward that stinking problem. Of course, there will always be roadblocks along the road to success, but stay definite on the course. Waving a flag of surrender is not an option! See only the checkered flag in the future.

Dream as if the impossible dream has already came true. A broken-winged angel can still sail and glide, maybe just not as high as she used to. So come on, believe in the positive dream. Who knows? The end result very well could be a superhero in someone else's eyes.

# 40

## That Voice Inside

The "keeper of the stars" knows that they must align perfectly to possibly hear that voice deep inside. It is the one that tells you to be on the lookout because this very well could be the soul mate that satisfies your every emotional and spiritual need. Suffering from sleep loss and restlessness and having giddy feelings are obvious signs that you may have a crush someone that you have been praying to come along. This is the one that makes your heart do a flip-flop and leap up to the heavens. You may experience a feeling of sprouting wings because your feet do feel as though they never touch the ground.

You may have been lost and searching all your for that unique someone who will make the fireworks more colorful and make the nighttime stars seem more brilliant. Laughing together at the same silly jokes and sharing the same kind of dedicated faith lets you know that dreams are truly possible. You believe in each other and know that you are each other's destiny. Angels have come together as one powerful force to rescue your lonely, drowning soul.

You may feel very dissatisfied, however, if you do not confess to that one person that he or she has given you hopeful emotions and that you are "sweet" on that person. So wish upon a shooting star, dream as if you are the main character in the fairy tale, and exist like this is the last day on this planet.

Listen to that screaming voice inside because it may offer deeply felt love, affection, and the fondness of someone never quite known before.

# 41

## The American Indian

In life, we sometimes must show the bravery of the American Indian. We must reveal courage during our battles in this great experience we call life. Showing great valor during a life-altering death or when we ourselves look death straight in the eye will earn tremendous respect, while we try to recover from our many tears of sorrow. Keeping the chin up and being proud and confident can give others inspiration that may be much needed.

Facing that adversity head-on, like soldiers do with the enemy, will prove to be bold and superhero-like. Having an unusually daring spirit, can only move us forward, if it is used in the right way. Some days will be very frustrating and tiresome, but we must continue on that journey and hold our heads high.

Laughter can often let us be less mindful of the challenge we have before us. It helps shake the heaviness off our shoulders. Unaware, we might not even notice the Devil or the adversity that is coming straight toward us. But that guy is sneaky and corrupt like that. The manner in which we choose to react to his underhanded ways does matter, though.

When we think positive, our bodies will follow. Be magnificent and go that extra mile. We must get our bravery on, like the American Indian. And who knows? We may just hear the angels applaud us for a job well done, up in the distant clouds.

# 42

## The Gut Doesn't Lie

Gut-wrenching twists and turns usually means something is fishy, and it often doesn't lie. Misleading souls can make one question his own intelligence and make them feel lost and empty. Asking yourself question after question and running things through a worried, fearful mind can make your soul begin to scream! Hearing that little voice on your shoulder may give you a pounding headache and should be a yellow caution flag for an uncertain mind and unsettled stomach.

Be extremely careful because all demons will be in disguise and will create an uneasiness. Even using an expensive calculator doesn't even quite make things add up. Pumping ideas through your heart and mind can make you feel insane until the truth comes tumbling out. Hopefully, the heart will be out of dangerous territory when the ammo is unloaded, which can leave you feeling shell-shocked.

Having a distrustful, suspicious mind and queasy stomach should always be a clear warning sign that something isn't right because the gut doesn't usually lie.

# 43

# The Smell of
# BBQ on the Grill

Tempting and appealing are the smells of BBQ on the grill in the middle of a long, cold winter, as we anticipate the charcoal-grilled taste. First, we are born into the tender seasoning of learning to walk and talk the BBQ lingo. Finally, when the fires of the teenage years die down, the coals can be left attended for a short bit.

Forecasting only enjoyable temperatures and bathing in the good faith of our Lord, we grow uncontrollably, like weeds, in the hot sunlight. It now becomes time to marry the sauce to the favorable meat on the grill. What a heavenly duo and pair! Living free and loving the BBQ life that we have been given is more than we can barely eat. As the sauce cooks in, we relax in the cool, gentle breeze. Making the cooks proud, they predict their future as an outstanding barbeque chefs.

Side dishes are a welcome gift brought to the family picnic. Desserts are a long-awaited dream and hopeful plan. Activities such as volleyball, fishing, and croquet fill the long, eventful day at the picnic. After an abundance of playtime, a much-needed nap is taken in the shade.

Heaven is the location of the next family barbeque. Just imagine the sweet aroma of BBQ on the grill that the angels will have prepared for us, when we enter our family reunion at the golden gates of heaven.

# 44

## *Two Peas in a Pod*

Two people sharing a likeness and friendship are often called two peas in pod. Real friends value the worth of each other's company. Close friends share a chuckle or giggle; only they know what's so funny by the expression on the other's face. The United States Postal Service is commonly used to add a little sunshine to another's day with a delivery of a smiling card or note.

Friendships can provide a sense of belonging and family. Dynamic duos can also be sisters, cousins, or brothers. Friends or family are "there" for a mourning heart or for just a little touch of orneriness. We need each other terribly and can pull the best from one another. We are all unique individuals, and we have little or no time for comparing one another.

We definitely need each other, especially, when our laundry basket gets dumped upside down. Faithful pets are frequently our best, loyal friends. They won't talk back, disagree, or have any of the worst human flaws. We also must realize the importance of a friend who equals our pure spirituality and positive, influential qualities.

So when someone says, "You're two peas in a pod," be proud, relax, and say, "Thank you!"

# 45

## We All Have Some Form of Handicap

We all have some form of handicap, big or small. So we most show compassion for our fellow man. Being cautious of others' feelings is a sign of having Jesus in our thoughts, actions, and heart. Perhaps our handicap is as simple as cursing or even having a negative, damaging attitude. Sometimes, it may be a hearing loss, a speech impediment, or even a loss of a limb. Possibly, we have forgotten to have sympathy for someone who has felt the emptiness of a once-shared home after an unexpected, sudden death of a loved one. It is our choice to have mercy upon another's soul. For example, when our children stumble, fall, and suffer an injury, our hearts go out to them.

Don't let your fears keep you from the tenderness of a relationship with another soul. Be prepared because it just might turn out to be your handicap. So, if you're thinking that you are "all that," think again.

Today doesn't know what tomorrow may bring us, so go ahead—be the captain of your own ship! Don't let the heart be kept on a high shelf. Have a rich compassion for others because we all have some form of handicap, big or small.

# 46

# The Wicked Witch of the South

Anyone who must encounter the path of the "wicked witch of the South" takes the risky chance of being chewed up, spit up, and left for dead, for all she cares. Miss Evilness is called the premenstrual cycle. Like an unpredictable spring storm, funnel clouds and spitting hail may occur at any given moment. The mentality of a woman suffering from that untamed syndrome cannot forecast an uncontrollable shower of tears that can darken a sun-filled day. She can rain profusely on a picnic or parade, and she can totally soak an event that you have been eagerly anticipating.

Caution! Don't be stuck down in a ditch when her flood waters rush through, creating a new geological pathway. The consequences of expressing the wrong choice of words may have to be both suffered and lived with. A wishful feeling of death is a fair thought. What will her raging emotions possibly think of next? Her ugly, wart-invaded head formulates an uneasiness and weakness for her surrounding people, who possibly feel that this very well could be the end of mankind.

God cries as the storm passes. All the angels sigh with relief when they realize she was only a temporarily broken-winged sister. Nothing lasts forever, except God's everlasting and understanding love. That week from hell has finally passed, with survivors who beat the odds of the coming of the "wicked-witch of the South." Thank God!

# 47

# *Working a Puzzle*

Confusion is similar to working a jigsaw puzzle. Scratching your head as a chicken scratches at the ground is what you may feel sometimes. Some indecisive people will say one thing and then do another. Clarification is what is really needed in these troubling days. Patience and temperance are the most frequent tests that you will endure. Spending a vast amount of time, pondering if the direction or the decision is correct, can be baffling, to say the least.

Remaining undecided or playing the guessing game can make you feel as if you are going bonkers. Nerves and senses can be shredded apart and will let the loaded stress beat them down like a hard, pounding rain. Mysterious phantoms shadow what you know to be true. Quality time is lost while searching for a definite answer. Leaving no stones unturned, you toss around right and wrong ideas.

Praying for the right answer and weighing the pros and cons becomes the building blocks for a solution, which seems to take an eternity to get to. Your mind can only withstand limited force winds before it comes shattering down, like glass falling on tile flooring.

Finally, a sigh of relief after a sweet ending has made its final resting place on a once-confused mind. The last piece of puzzle has been found.

# 48

## The Only Directions

$\mathcal{U}$p and forward are the only directions, if willpower is present in your life. Having a definite, stubborn mind-set will make your decision, if success will be awarded to you or not. Mentally, you must desire the outcome for which you are struggling for. Mind tricks can be the enemy, if you aren't extremely cautious. Determination will have to be a "prescribed medicine" taken daily. Striving to be 100% in every situation, can be a complete and utter undertaking. Having a cheerful, positive outlook and attitude can only help the situation, though. Attempting an endeavor and falling down is never a crime. However, never even trying may put you in "prison" for life. Designing your life around the predicament at hand, can offer you a head start on the bigger-than-life problem. Authorizing negative thoughts will not promote strength and toughness. Keeping a tight "cap on" controlling negative thoughts, sets the mind in "go" mode or in the "on" position. Staying charged with electricity, will keep the lights burning bright. Fixing your mental status to never be overpowered by a "pothole" in the road of life, is what must be done to accomplish your goals. Of course, you will experience agony and grief, along this rocky highway they call life. But having the ability and the blessing to look at life in only two directions, up and forward, will give you the possibility of a true-life success story.

# 49

## The Lone Wolf

Loneliness can make your soul scream and ache. Where would you be without a life companion? Friendship can be carried across a rock-bedded creek if need to be, but your isolated heart longs for an embracing soulmate. Money and material things can leave you empty, miserable and feeling vacant inside. Your heart bleeds for another heart to hold. The participation of someone who will caress your solitary spirit when it cries out. Maybe to keep your feet warm or to be able to lie on that someone special's shoulder at night. Being stuck down deep in a ditch or running scared, only makes this problem grow into a giant, that can't climb down from the beanstalk, because of a weight issue. Shooting stars may offer hope to some people, though. Being a "single" soul doesn't mean that you are damaged or defective either. The night-time stars that glisten, just haven't aligned yet. The "keeper" will align them perfectly, light the path to someone else's heart, and unload your weight-filled shoulders. Dust off your heart, that's been kept on the top shelf of the closet, for safe keeping, and it will be gently opened to a tender partner, who will forever be your mate. The lone wolf won't be alone any longer. Soon, you both will be howling at the glowing, full-moon, together.

# 50

## A Ton of Bricks

You can live your life with a feeling of resentment against another, but it will weigh you down, heavy, like a ton of bricks. After we forgive someone, though, your "load" will feel as light as a floating, blue-sky cloud. It will not be easy setting someone "free" from your judgement. Relieving all their wrong doings will release all feeling of ill-will towards them and can create you to have real empathetic feelings, instead. Pardoning someone who has made you question your own intelligence, must happen. Sometimes people try to "steal" your well-being and frequently even your happiness. Perhaps, or an act that has changed your perfect and polished life. Maybe a false rumor that has been viciously started, that altered your life for the darker. After going to your priest or pastor, he absolves your sins, if you are truly sorry for them. Give up the hard feelings, the heavy anger towards someone. Pray for that one, who has given you the grief. Jesus even asked for forgiveness for His persecutors, for they do not know what they do. You may never know when you may be asking for forgiveness from someone in your life. Maybe, then you can lighten that heavy load, that feels like a ton of bricks.

Printed in the United States
By Bookmasters